The New SPELL-WELL

Book 2

C J Ridout

NELSON

Nelson Blackie
Westercleddens Road
Bishopbriggs
Glasgow
G64 2NZ UK

Thomas Nelson and Sons Ltd
Nelson House Mayfield Road
Walton-on-Thames Surrey
KT12 5PL UK

© Blackie and Son Ltd 1978

First published by Blackie and Son Ltd 1978
ISBN 0-216-90614-8

This edition published by Thomas Nelson and Sons Ltd
1993

ISBN 0-17-424554-8
NPN 9 8 7 6 5 4 3

To help you learn the words in this book
1 Say the word
2 Look at the word
3 Trace the word
4 Write without copying
5 Check
6 Make your own dictionary—write all
  the words you learn in it

The Alphabet (26 letters)
CAPITALS
A B C D E F G H I J K L M
N O P Q R S T U V W X Y Z

small letters
a b c d e f g h i j k l m
n o p q r s t u v w x y z

The Vowels (5 letters)
a e i o u

The Consonants (21 letters)
b c d f g h j k l m n
p q r s t v w x y z
(all the alphabet except the vowels)

1

1	2	3
bay	mow	born
lay	row	horn
gay	crow	torn
pray	sow	morning

4	5	6
sea	shy	few
seat	spy	dew
meat	why	new
neat	fry	news

7	8	9
scrub	nail	tie
screw	pail	pie
scratch	tail	lie
scrap	sail	tied

10	11	12
tailor	any	this
sailor	many	that
sailed	after	these
sailing	before	those

Guy Fawkes' Night

paper	night	roasted
sticks	sky	collected
rubbish	stars	gathered
branches	moon	built
wood	fireworks	lit
tyre	sparkler	guarded
bonfire	rocket	screamed
barrow	potatoes	shouted
trousers	sausages	exclaimed
jacket	toffee	gasped
anorak		
scarf	deafening	brightly
gloves	terrifying	carefully
guy	glowing	fiercely
matches	dazzling	loudly
flames	blinding	excitedly
smoke	bright	nervously

Phrases

flames shot up	jumping jack
the sparks flew	Roman candle
roar, crackle, hiss	a sudden bang
leaning dangerously	bright orange
Catherine wheel	shooting upwards
roasting chestnuts	November the fifth

3

1	**2**	**3**
came	hop	bone
same	shop	alone
shame	crop	stone
blame	chop	cone

4	**5**	**6**
hall	fix	rude
wall	fox	rule
small	axe	ruled
tall	tax	June

7	**8**	**9**
pink	eat	loss
link	treat	gloss
shrink	beat	cross
wink	bleat	toss

10	**11**	**12**
frame	fail	put
became	trail	push
game	mail	pull
tame	pail	bull

The Postman

letter	bell	deliver
postcard	bicycle	collect
airmail	gate	give
envelope	home	ring
paper	smile	wait
stamp	house	read
post office	flat	write
mail	round	seal
mail van	duty	stick
postbox	uniform	open
parcel		
bag	heavy	sharply
sack	friendly	loudly
bundle	busy	clearly
letterbox	cold	slowly
delivery	regular	quickly

Phrases

ring the bell

heavy bag

a birthday card

pleasant surprise

parcel post

addressed to me

Christmas card

a registered parcel

a postal order

at the window

red postbox

early in the morning

second delivery

stuck firmly

5

1	**2**	**3**
real	sir	lake
deal	stir	rake
meal	shirt	wake
steal	third	sake

4	**5**	**6**
few	glow	felt
blew	bow	belt
chew	lower	pelt
grew	owner	melt

7	**8**	**9**
nose	side	hare
note	wide	fare
vote	ride	spare
wrote	pride	share

10	**11**	**12**
fold	time	take
gold	wine	rake
sold	line	snake
told	shine	shake

A Cat and Dog Fight

fur
paws
claws
teeth
pursuit
bark
pavement
tree
branch
neighbours
ladder
bird
kitten
tail
safety
Alsatian

terrified
frightened
angry
panic-stricken
huge
sharp
scared

galloped
raced
snarled
pursued
bit
growled
climbed
rescued

spit
leapt
darted
crawled
mewed
scrambled
hunted
yelped
prowled

fiercely
quickly
speedily
gingerly
stealthily
peacefully

Phrases

bright green eyes
claws like needles
climbed to safety
with arched back
   and bristling fur
tail waving angrily
disturb the peace

bared his teeth
in hot pursuit
nine lives of a cat
on the scent
a menacing growl
sprang like lightning
tail between his legs

1	2	3
tire	mile	bill
fire	smile	kill
five	while	chill
drive	pile	drill

4	5	6
hang	mess	hip
rang	less	whip
sang	bless	ship
sprang	press	clip

7	8	9
weak	dwell	like
beak	swell	strike
speak	smell	bike
leak	shell	hike

10	11	12
who	use	park
whom	abuse	bark
whose	used	hard
lose	refuse	yard

A Visit to the Circus

animal

horse

lion

elephant

seal

audience

juggler

clown

acrobat

lion-tamer

ringmaster

trapeze

costume

ticket

rider

tent

cage

trick

ring

caravan

safety-net

whip

procession

parade

dance

small

huge

excited

daring

silly

clever

intelligent

strong

funny

colourful

balance

swing

climb

jump

hang

ride

cycle

perform

tumble

crack

clap

cheer

trot

dangerously

skilfully

bravely

gracefully

Phrases

glittering costumes

loud applause

tightrope walker

a dangerous stunt

lost his trousers

dizzy heights

snarled angrily

a human pyramid

the band struck up

a deathly hush

9

1	2	3
too	such	go
tool	much	goes
cool	duchess	going
fool	duke	gone

4	5	6
our	ash	feel
hour	dash	heel
flour	crash	wheel
sour	splash	steel

7	8	9
fur	do	rent
purse	does	lent
nurse	doing	dent
turnip	done	tent

10	11	12
took	one	which
look	once	what
hook	two	why
hood	twice	where

A Birthday Party

present
parcel
postman
invitation
games
football
skipping rope
balloons
parents
friends
cake
candles
sandwiches
sausages
jelly
ice cream
trifle

watch
bicycle
jigsaw
book
doll
beads
camera
marbles
pencil case

interesting
useful
tasty
disappointing
beautiful
lovely
broken

unwrap
open
play
enjoy
break
eat
drink
cut
taste
sing
find
light

happily
joyfully
tearfully
together

Phrases

a pleasant surprise
many happy returns
another year older
party clothes
six o'clock
"Happy Birthday"

musical chairs
hunt the thimble
a knock at the door
snakes and ladders
blind man's buff
plenty to eat

1	2	3
rate	lark	rush
grate	shark	brush
date	dark	crush
hate	mark	hush

4	5	6
been	fir	deck
queen	firm	neck
screen	first	peck
sixteen	thirst	speck

7	8	9
lamp	aid	cow
damp	laid	now
tramp	mail	how
cramp	rail	brown

10	11	12
eve	wear	above
even	pear	below
lever	bear	other
evening	tear	another

A Village

road
cottage
thatch
roof
roofs
farmhouse
signpost
crossroads
church
porch
belfry
tower
steeple
farmer
lane
wayside
village shop

inn
hedge
chimney
market
school
pond
river
field
animals

attractive
pretty
friendly
ancient
colourful
quiet
contented

stroll
climb
ramble
ring
shout
plod
work
gather
gossip
smoke
rest
bleat
bellow
drive
wander
plough
travel

Phrases

the village green
old stone church
the belfry tower
old, ruined mill
five-barred gate
an evening stroll

the market place
old-fashioned garden
down by the river
shouts of the children
at the Village Hall
off the motorway

1	**2**	**3**
wild	fond	wise
mild	pond	rise
child	beyond	like
children	bond	strike

4	**5**	**6**
bath	trip	mate
path	trap	plate
father	strip	state
rather	strap	skate

7	**8**	**9**
bean	past	stoop
lean	cast	stool
clean	mast	school
jeans	master	wool

10	**11**	**12**
grew	key	goose
new	keys	geese
drew	donkey	tooth
stew	donkeys	teeth

Preparing for Christmas

preparation
pudding
flour
raisin
sultana
currant
turkey
sausage
apple
orange
cake
icing
fairy lights
marzipan
decoration
holly
mistletoe

present
secret
surprise
excitement
happiness
cards
carols
crackers
tinsel
flowers

sweet
many
sticky
scarlet
large
small

bright
glad
steaming
expensive
plentiful
gay
joyful
spicy
enough

prepare
bake
stir
weigh
expect
gather
receive

Phrases

decorate the tree
the finishing touch
anxious to help
a bulky parcel
an iced cake
wrapping paper

"A Merry Christmas"
to hang paper chains
the last day at school
at the top of the tree
Father Christmas
clear, frosty air

1	**2**	**3**
high	cave	leaf
sigh	wave	leaves
sight	shave	lead
night	slave	plead

4	**5**	**6**
each	sheet	wade
teach	steep	trade
beach	street	fade
reach	sheep	shade

7	**8**	**9**
wife	care	smoke
life	mare	joke
lives	scare	choke
strife	square	spoke

10	**11**	**12**
pave	ease	yesterday
gave	please	today
save	tease	tonight
brave	weasel	tomorrow

Winter

season
football
netball
hail
frost
sledge
skis
overcoat
scarf
gloves
icicle
weather
fog
ice
snowman
snowball
snowdrift

blizzard
warmth
chestnut
fuel
squirrel
robin

cold
bare
leafless
icy
slippery
cloudy
clear
foggy
wet
frosty

glittering
damp
blue
numb
dreary
white
grey

freeze
froze
skate
slide
thaw
harden
shiver
pity
stamp

Phrases

a white world
hanging icicles
bitterly cold
icy blast
blazing fire
blue with cold

the first snowdrop
the leafless trees
biting east wind
sledging down the hill
wet, miserable night
just around the corner

1	**2**	**3**
head	sack	bare
bread	slack	fare
dead	rack	glare
lead	crack	stare

4	**5**	**6**
oak	brain	sweep
soak	chain	cheek
cloak	grain	feed
croak	train	bleed

7	**8**	**9**
see	ice	sick
seed	spice	stick
deer	nice	brick
queer	slice	chicken

10	**11**	**12**
carry	more	raid
carries	tore	laid
carried	store	paid
carriage	score	afraid

The Lost Puppy

coat
tail
paws
ears
collar
address
disc
tongue
lead
slipper
bone
biscuit
bowl
master
mistress
stranger
reward
basket
kennel

friendly
sad
tasty
smooth
rough
beautiful
homeless
alert
watchful
faithful
thankful

licked
barked
cried
jumped
wagged
romped
cowered

played
slept
chewed
gnawed
walked
ate
bathed
brushed
combed

hungrily
comfortably
soundly
peacefully
pleadingly
gently
happily
hopefully
gratefully

Phrases
cocked his head
wagged his tail
barked loudly
found his master

lay contentedly
jumped excitedly
growled angrily
joyful reunion

19

1	**2**	**3**
goat	find	suck
goal	wind	struck
coal	rind	pluck
foal	grind	tuck

4	**5**	**6**
pick	oil	might
quick	boil	light
tick	soil	tight
lick	spoil	bright

7	**8**	**9**
word	straw	should
work	claw	would
world	law	could
worth	lawn	shoulder

10	**11**	**12**
kept	claim	here
wept	reclaim	there
swept	main	along
crept	remain	across

Caught—Stealing Apples

fence
mischief
trouble
bag
rascal
temptation
fruit
branch
direction
packet
trick
stick
culprit
behaviour
policeman
punishment

delicious
sweet
juicy
favourite
honest
artful
hungry
unwise
stealthy
angry
miserable
wrong
severe
naughty
sour
ripe

pass
tempt
climb
clamber
catch
notice
scramble
surround
warn
steal
seize
munch
pursue
escape
dodge
release

Phrases

a gruff voice
to scale a wall
tempting fruit
not far away
close on their heels
a cunning trick
catch sight of

overhanging bough
failed to notice
filled their pockets
a shower of apples
a warning shout
neighbouring farm
an upset stomach

1	2	3
coin	hay	shout
join	way	stout
joint	lay	scout
point	stray	trout

4	5	6
team	weed	blow
steam	need	throw
stream	heed	blown
scream	freed	thrown

7	8	9
wore	range	hunt
bore	change	stunt
sore	strange	blunt
core	danger	shunt

10	11	12
round	door	none
ground	floor	few
found	blood	some
pound	flood	plenty

Journey into Space

rocket
motors
control
screen
countdown
planet
gravity
universe
Mars
link-up
transmitter
oxygen
telescope
parachute
commander
pilot
instruments

astronaut
fuel
stars
explosion
helmet
visor
spacesuit

weightless
frightening
eerie
bright
deafening
blinding
gleaming
flaming
distant

ordered
launched
landed
crashed
steered
fired
adjusted
contacted
crouched
orbited

suddenly
smoothly
carefully
swiftly
uncomfortably
friendly

Phrases

multi-stage rocket
floating in space
space station
deathly silence
huge craters
contacted base

lift off
safety harness
strange creatures
return to Earth
splash down
a collision course

1	**2**	**3**
arch	loud	off
starch	proud	cliff
march	cloud	stiff
larch	count	stuff

4	**5**	**6**
shake	tint	broke
shape	print	stroke
grape	sprint	poke
scrape	hint	coke

7	**8**	**9**
won	join	gift
wonder	joiner	sift
son	noise	swift
tonne	voice	rift

10	**11**	**12**
earn	loudly	front
learn	mount	back
early	mountain	beside
pearl	fountain	ahead

All the Fun of the Fair

stall
roundabout
dodgem-car
helter-skelter
rifle
big wheel
candy-floss
toffee-apple
coconut shy
bingo
music
swings
moon rocket
fortune-teller
goldfish
hoopla
caravan
money

target
bull's-eye
prize
cobweb
skeleton
lights

dizzy
lucky
unlucky
eerie
frightened
ugly
skinny
dark
colourful
bright
sticky

spend
shoot
miss
hit
win
try
drive
aim
buy
lick
eat
tickle
stagger
shout
yell
cry
laugh
scream

Phrases

tell your fortune
hall of mirrors
blare of music
excited screams
bump the dodgems

test your strength
howls of laughter
roll up, roll up !
win a goldfish
whizz round

25

1	2	3
bound	waste	tick
sound	haste	tock
round	taste	clock
found	paste	o'clock

4	5	6
ditch	gather	dance
pitch	together	France
stitch	other	glance
switch	mother	chance

7	8	9
foam	moth	town
soap	broth	brown
roar	cloth	crown
board	clothes	drown

10	11	12
ditches	month	own
switches	Monday	blown
witches	money	shown
stitches	monkey	flown

The Police

city	law	watch
town	order	direct
road	helmet	protect
crossroads	uniform	help
pavement	baton	guard
traffic	protection	steal
walkie-talkie	constable	drive
patrol car	detective	stop
motorway	criminal	outwit
people		
crowd	blue	always
football match	tall	never
thief	strong	
prison	helpful	morning
jail	watchful	afternoon
escape	brave	evening
chase	busy	night

Phrases

keep order
arrest a thief
preventing crime
ask the way
police headquarters
all night long

direct the traffic
outside the school
protecting property
navy blue uniform
police dog handler
pair of handcuffs

1	**2**	**3**
pie	sing	pure
tie	cling	sure
die	fling	cure
died	wing	demure

4	**5**	**6**
file	fort	foe
stile	port	hoe
tile	sport	toe
Nile	report	doe

7	**8**	**9**
pour	blue	water
four	flue	wasp
fourteen	glue	want
mourn	true	wall

10	**11**	**12**
east	down	our
beast	clown	your
feast	frown	their
least	gown	its

Rescued from Pirates

ship	enormous	boarded
prisoner	vicious	led
captain	horrible	stood
beard	torn	escaped
hair	ugly	attacked
fight	untidy	ordered
eye	dirty	captured
scar	heavy	fought
weapon	sharp	killed
pistol	cowardly	jumped
cutlass	ragged	shouted
belt	cruel	floated
dagger	blood-curdling	
gunpowder	ruthless	bravely
cabin	rough	suddenly
bunk	frightened	fiercely
treasure	fierce	desperately
chest	friendly	cautiously

Phrases

taken aboard	a cruel laugh
skull and crossbones	a black patch
panic-stricken	walk the plank
bloodthirsty crew	put in irons
gang of pirates	ship ahoy !

Word Game—Rule One

When you play any game you have to obey certain rules.

Look at these words:

win	winning	can	canned
thin	thinner	wet	wettest
hid	hidden	fit	fitting

Notice that each short word has

a. *one* consonant at the end.

b. *one vowel* before that consonant.

See what has happened when you add –ing, –er, –est, –ed, –en.

This gives you the First Rule of the game, telling you when to double the last consonant.

Round 1 Pick out those words which double the last consonant when you add –ing:

chop	rub	bend	rob
print	skip	spin	spend

Round 2 Pick out those words which double the last consonant when you add –est:

hot	black	sad	dim
thick	flat	warm	strong

A Rainy Day

raindrop	heavy	drip
puddle	light	fall
pool	rushing	drizzle
gutter	damp	trickle
dribble	continuous	lash
window-pane	beating	drench
shower	dreary	soak
storm	cloudy	splash
downpour	grey	burst
gale	steady	flood
umbrella	waterproof	flow
raincoat	muddy	stream
wellingtons	sodden	pour
anorak	soaked	glisten
rainbow	miserable	hurry
reflection	dismal	wear
thunderstorm	comfortable	shelter

Phrases

leaden skies	drip, drip, drip
an April shower	steady downpour
thirsty plants	driving rain
across the sky	dancing raindrops
a dreary day	flooded road
dirty puddles	sun breaks through

31

Word Game—Rule Two

Look at these words :

fast	faster	plant	planted
cheap	cheapest	climb	climbing

Notice that each short word

a. ends in two consonants, *or*

b. ends in two vowels and a consonant.

In each longer word the endings are added without doubling the end consonant. This gives you the Second Rule.

Round 3   Which of these words do not double the end consonant when –ed is added ?

weed	dart	stop	crack
fit	clap	fear	pass

Round 4   Which of these words do not double the end consonant when –er is added ?

fat	cold	swim	weak
grand	stop	kind	warm

Round 5   Which of these words obey Rule One and which obey Rule Two when –ing is added ?

drum	tell	let	send
warm	wet	jump	slip

Horses

mare	bit	shoe
stallion	rein	own
foal	saddle	trot
pony	harness	carry
master	stirrup	whip
mistress	blacksmith	remember
meadow	horseshoe	jump
farm	hoof	prance
stable	groom	neigh
straw		graze
coat	young	gallop
tail	handsome	canter
mane	kind	
sugar	devoted	cleverly
oats	cruel	willingly
bridle	ill-treated	intelligently
hands	heavy	prettily

Phrases

large, airy stable	carefully groomed
to "break-in" a colt	touch of the rein
work with a will	nibble the grass
whinnied softly	gallop across the field
a heavy load	
long, flowing mane	enter a gymkhana

33

Word Game—Exercises

Apply Rule One to these words:

1 Add –ing	**2** Add –er	**3** Add –est	**4** Add –ed
pat	sup	fat	pat
clap	chop	wet	pot
skip	rob	sad	stop
cut	win	big	slip
run	hop	dim	trim
swim	thin	mad	whip
spin	fat	thin	rub
shut	shop	hot	scrub

Apply Rule Two to these words:

5 Add –ing	**6** Add –er	**7** Add –est	**8** Add –en
stamp	plant	grand	thick
tell	bank	swift	dark
send	talk	strong	black
mend	lend	fond	less
drink	spend	cold	chick
call	sing	bold	gold
start	read	kind	fall
mark	dust	wild	sharp

A Visit to a Farm

animal
horse
hen
duck
turkey
goose
gosling
chicken
sheep
lamb
calf
calves
sheepdog
wheat
potato
cabbage
turnip

corn
farm worker
tractor
field
barn
furrow
fertiliser

tired
weary
happy
cheerful
hungry
healthy
interesting
fertile
fallow

work
toil
sow
reap
thresh
gather
graze
plough
harvest
rear
neigh
bleat
gobble
bark
frolic
gambol
shear

Phrases

dairy cows
do the milking
collect the milk
   churns
lowing cattle
playful lambs

picturesque farm-
   house
combine harvester
away in the fields
neighbouring village
faithful watchdog

Another Word Game

This game is called Adding –ful or –fully

| tear | tearful | tearfully |

When you add **full** to another word, one of the l's is dropped, but when you add **fully** both l's remain.

grace	graceful	gracefully
joy	joyful	joyfully
play	playful	playfully
care	careful	carefully
pain	painful	painfully
faith	faithful	faithfully
use	useful	usefully
fear	fearful	fearfully
wonder	wonderful	wonderfully
spoon	spoonful	—
mouth	mouthful	—

Exercise   **Add –ful to these words :**

peace	sin	hand
thank	dread	truth
cheer	waste	art

Lost in the Hills

boots	wind	tramped
anorak	rain	climbed
compass	snow	hiked
map	cloud	clambered
rucksack	mist	wandered
pocket	fog	shouted
bracken		rested
heather	marshy	rescued
flask	icy	dropped
sandwiches	desolate	descended
direction	rolling	
darkness	heavy	happily
visibility	tired	swiftly
sight	exhausted	strongly
slope	frozen	hoarsely
mountain	welcome	wearily
valley	dangerous	thankfully
rocks	exciting	sleepily

Phrases

a terrifying experi-
  ence
a sudden blizzard
darkness fell
a cold, damp mist

a biting wind
huddled together
a distant cry
waved frantically
a rescue party

Words that Sound Alike

blew	threw	new
blue	through	knew
fair	bare	hare
fare	bear	hair
weak	beech	been
week	beach	bean
hole	bored	sow
whole	board	sew
flower	bow	aloud
flour	bough	allowed
meat	steel	peace
meet	steal	piece
break	stare	tale
brake	stair	tail
plane	way	ring
plain	weigh	wring
due	of	not
dew	off	knot

Road Accident

bicycle
bus
car
van
lorry
motor bike
street
crossing
crossroads
lights
ball
pavement
telephone
emergency
ambulance
doctor
nurse

stretcher
policeman
hospital
witness
driver
pedestrian
cyclist

fast
injured
dazed
wobbling
unsafe
racing
unconscious
shocked
bruised

kicked
fell
skidded
crashed
heard
moved
passed
carried
walked
broke
lay
helped

quickly
carelessly
carefully
heavily

Phrases

on my way to school
a screech of brakes
a shuddering halt
without looking
describe what
   happened

unable to move
at the roadside
dialled 999
rushed to the spot
safety first
a sudden crash

Shortened Words

I'll	I will	isn't	is not
we'll	we will	can't	cannot
I've	I have	there's	there is
we've	we have	it's	it is
o'er	over	'tis	it is

Girls' Names

Elizabeth	Catherine	Christine
Margaret	Susan	Victoria
Mary	Jennifer	Anne

Boys' Names

Peter	David	John
Michael	Charles	Robert
Paul	William	James

Silent Letters

know	hour	lamb	answer
kneel	honest	limb	sword
knock	scissors	thumb	wrist
knit	scene	crumb	wrong
knife	sign	bomb	wreck

The Sea

ocean
waves
depth
wind
storm
gale
breakers
tide
harbour
ship
yacht
lighthouse
lifeboat
buoy
anchor
beach
coast

seagull
sailor
fisherman
seaweed
sand
rocks
pebbles
whirlpool

calm
rough
stormy
high
angry
rolling
blue
deep

ripple
rock
crash
upset
wreck
spray
shelter
sail
bathe
toss
stretch
ebb
flow
carry
float
fish
water ski

Phrases

the drenching spray
cry of the seagulls
a fierce storm
ebb of the tide
rippling over the
    sandy beach

white horses
stretches far and
    wide
ride the waves
dash against the
    rocks

41

Flowers

daisy	dandelion	rose
tulip	cornflower	lily
pansy	daffodil	poppy
snowdrop	primrose	marigold

Fruits

pear	apple	strawberry
plum	orange	gooseberry
grape	banana	raspberry
peach	lemon	blackberry

Vegetables

potato	bean	cauliflower
carrot	beetroot	turnip
cabbage	leek	lettuce
parsnip	peas	onion

Our Relatives

mother	daughter	sister
father	son	brother
aunt	cousin	niece
uncle	grandfather	nephew

Small Boat Adventure

oars
yacht
sail
dinghy
rowing boat
shore
misfortune
difficulty
accident
plight
despair
weariness
island
current
doctor
canoe

calm
difficult
rough
naughty
skilled
brave
sudden
frightened
grasp
lucky

immediately
instantly
fortunately
surprisingly
finally

dare
untie
moor
steer
drift
capsize
dive
plunge
clamber
clutch
attempt
shriek
shout
revive
paddle
swim

Phrases

gust of wind
cry for help
full of energy
feeling of despair
warning shouts
a vain attempt
safe and sound

terrified cries
with great difficulty
an unattended boat
fine, sunny day
hoist the sail
calm waters of the
    lake

Colours

green	yellow	scarlet
blue	orange	red
black	brown	pink
white	cream	purple

Pets

horse	rabbit	donkey	budgie
tortoise	mouse	gerbil	hamster
pigeon	goat	cat	dog
parrot	guinea pig	kitten	puppy

The Weather

cloud	rainbow	storm
wind	sunshine	dew
frost	lightning	hail
snow	thunder	fog
rain	mist	drought

The Seasons

spring   summer   autumn   winter

Quiet Please! Somebody is Ill

illness
headache
disease
fever
bedroom
doctor
nurse
patient
medicine
pain
tonic
pulse
bruise
pill
hospital
ointment

operation
penicillin
measles
attack

infectious
feverish
pale
quiet
restless
painful
weak
sore
tired
healthy
poorly

fragile
serious
slight
comfortable
silent

complain
faint
examine
ache
cough
suffer
revive
prepare
recover
collapse

Phrases

a severe chill
careful nurse
call the doctor
very anxious
pale and weak
kind inquiries
a dose of medicine

walking on tip-toe
a slight attack of . . .
visit the patient
getting better
quench his thirst
high temperature
vase of flowers

Days of the Week

Sunday   Tuesday   Friday
Monday   Wednesday   Saturday
               Thursday

Months of the Year

January   May   September
February   June   October
March   July   November
April   August   December

Numbers

one   eleven   thirty
two   twelve   forty
three   thirteen   fifty
four   fourteen   sixty
five   fifteen   seventy
six   sixteen   eighty
seven   seventeen   ninety
eight   eighteen   hundred
nine   nineteen   thousand
ten   twenty   million